YOUR KNOWLEDGE HAS VALUE

AF145756

- We will publish your bachelor's and master's thesis, essays and papers

- Your own eBook and book - sold worldwide in all relevant shops

- Earn money with each sale

Upload your text at www.GRIN.com
and publish for free

Bibliographic information published by the German National Library:

The German National Library lists this publication in the National Bibliography; detailed bibliographic data are available on the Internet at http://dnb.dnb.de .

Imprint:

Copyright © 2017 GRIN Verlag, Open Publishing GmbH
Print and binding: Books on Demand GmbH, Norderstedt Germany
ISBN: 9783668456570

This book at GRIN:

http://www.grin.com/en/e-book/366936/introduction-into-microeconomics

Mike G.

Introduction into Microeconomics

GRIN Publishing

GRIN - Your knowledge has value

Since its foundation in 1998, GRIN has specialized in publishing academic texts by students, college teachers and other academics as e-book and printed book. The website www.grin.com is an ideal platform for presenting term papers, final papers, scientific essays, dissertations and specialist books.

Visit us on the internet:

http://www.grin.com/

http://www.facebook.com/grincom

http://www.twitter.com/grin_com

Microeconomics[1]

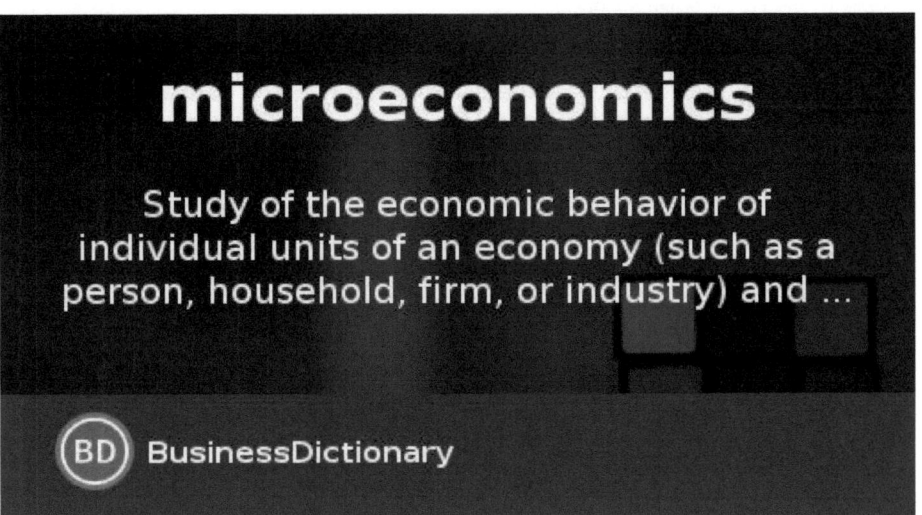

This text deals with the basic principles and theories of microeconomics. It describes the connection between demand and supply in perfect and imperfect markets to explain different, observed outcomes with the theoretical approaches. It is somewhat advanced to understand, therefore a certain level of knowledge about the market economy is recommended, but not absolutely necessary. In particular, market types like pure-competition, monopoly and monopolistic competition are mentioned and analyzed as well as cost minimization and profit maximization issues for each type. Various graphs underline the text and help to deliver and understand the message.

---

1   http://img.businessdictionary.com/share-social/terms/microeconomics.png

Content

Session One: A Simple Economic Model.

- **A simple economic model – The apartment market.**
  - A model is a simplification of the reality.
    - Question about whether it is good or not, no question about whether it is right or wrong.
      → Model has to be useful for your purpose.
  - Important in every model is to state which variables were exogenous and which are endogenous.
    - **Exogenous variables**: We take for given, do not explain them, just use them.
    - **Endogenous variables**: Outcome of the model, what we want to explain.
  - Two important instruments for the analysis of every model.
    - **Rationality**: Assumption that every individual will choose the best alternative.
    - **Concept of equilibrium**: Situation where nobody has incentive to change sth.; always search for an equilibrium and define what you need for this.

- **Perfect conditions market.**
  - **First Assumption**: All flats are homogeneous.
  - **Second Assumption**: The market contains a lot of landlords and renters.
  - **Exogenous variables**: Income of students, commuting costs, etc.
  - Creating the **demand curve** by asking for everybody's individual reservation price, the maximum amount of money willing to pay for a flat.
  - **Supply curve** is fully price-inelastic because in the short-run the amount of flats can't be increased or decreased.
    → Equilibrium at price p* where every student willing to pay the price will get a flat.
  - **Excess Demand**: More demand than supply (upward pressure on the price).
  - **Excess Supply**: More supply than demand (downward pressure on the price).
    => We just take the equilibrium for static,

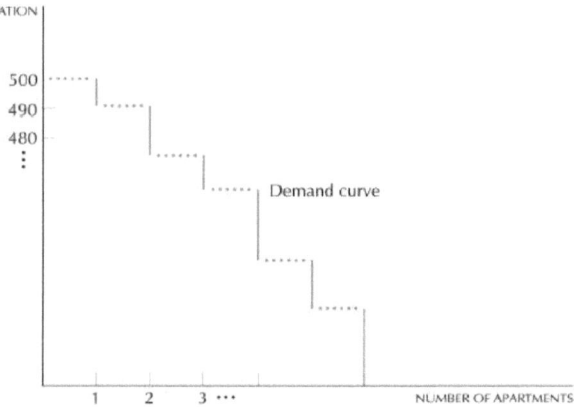

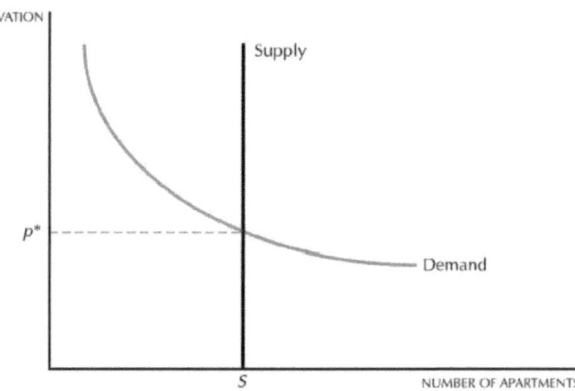

3

neglecting the dynamic processes.
- Distinct <u>demand</u> and <u>quantity demanded</u> (as well as <u>supply</u> and <u>quantity supplied</u>).
- Maybe because of a building project finished the amount of apartments supplied has suddenly increased.
  $\rightarrow$ Shift of the supply curve to the right, followed by movements on the demand curve because this still remains unchanged.
  $\rightarrow$ If the supply curve is inelastic, the consumers have to take the whole price effect by their owns.
- **Important information about this model.**
  - Market price: p^*
  - Who gets the flats? - The students with the highest reservation price.
  - Model is not "good" because some assumptions were not realistic.
    - **Rent control**: In modern metropolis' the government introduced price ceilings to prevent the rent prices to increase.
    - **Monopoly**: Often only big companies have the money to build new apartments and then control them. Assumption of a competitive market is not realistic.

- **Market with rent control.**
  - Price ceiling must be under the market equilibrium price p^*.
  - A price ceiling causes an excess demand, not every student willing to pay gets an apartment.
  - **Important information about this model.**
    - Market price: $p_{ceiling}$.
    - Who gets the flats? - The model can't tell anything about this.
      $\rightarrow$ Model is broken.

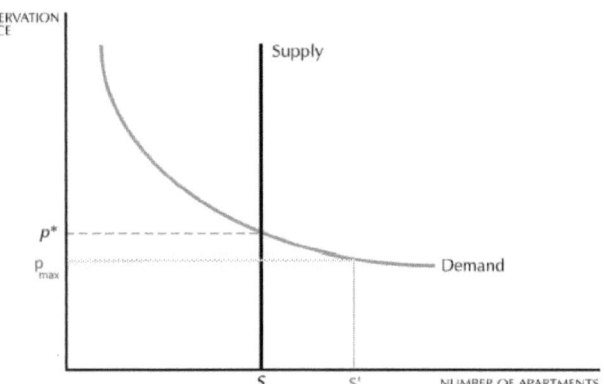

- **Monopoly.**
  - The monopolist wants to maximize his revenue.
  - Only possibility to increase the quantity demanded is to decrease prices.
    $\rightarrow$ Will also reduce the revenue.
  - Monopolist will calculate the optimal quantity supplied not with the demand curve, but with the marginal revenue curve.
    $\Rightarrow$ Optimal price is higher than p^* and will lead to some empty apartments.
    $\rightarrow$ Artificial scarcity is

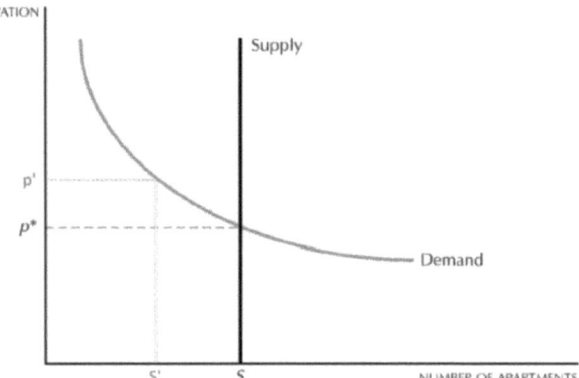

made.

- **Price-discriminating monopolist.**
  - Price-discrimination will solve the problem of artificial scarcity.
  - Suppose the monopolist knows the reservation price of every single consumer.
    → The monopolist will sell the same goods for different prices to maximize his revenue.
  - Sales manager at a local car distributor have to sell the car at this specific price, but will add bonuses like climate control, special warranty, etc. to increase the value of the car for the consumer and convince him to pay the price.
  - Amazon, e.g., gathered a lot of information about the buying behavior of his customers and adjusted prices to individuals reservation prices, with success.

- **Special tool to analyze the welfare of markets – Pareto efficiency.**
  - **Pareto efficiency**: No way to make one individual better off without making anyone else worse off.
  - **Perfect competition** is <u>Pareto efficient</u> because in the equilibrium you can make no-one better off without harming another one.
  - **Price ceiling** is <u>not</u> <u>Pareto efficient</u> because you can go to the black market and change renters and at least one person will be better off (if he/she values the flat more than the other former renter).
  - **Monopolist** is <u>not</u> <u>Pareto efficient</u> because some flats still remain empty and will improve the economic well-being if rented too.
  - **Perfectly-discriminatory monopolist** is <u>Pareto efficient</u> because everyone pays what he/she is willing to pay.

Session Two: Budget and Preferences.

- **Definition of Economics**: Economics is the science which studies human behavior as a relationship between ends and scarce means which have alternative uses.
  - Consumers want to achieve goals, but only have scarce resources with alternative uses to do so.
- Without scarcity Economics is not needed, scarcity is expressed by budged (here: money).
- Dealing with the problems of the consumers.
  - How much do they afford (budget).
  - What do they want (preferences).

- **Budget.**
  - Formalization of Budget B: $\{(x_1, x_2) \mid p_1 * x_1 + p_2 * x_2 \le m, x_1 \ge 0, x_2 \ge 0\}$
    - Each tuple consists of a combination of products x_1 and x_2.
    - Sum of price multiplied with amount of x_1 and price multiplied with amount of x_2 has to be lower or equal to the income m → Possibility to buy is limited to budget.
    - Neither x_1 nor x_2 can be negative numbers.
  - Turn into an equation: $p_1 * x_1 + p_2 * x_2 = m$

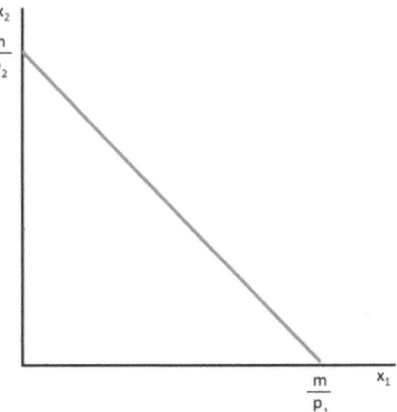

- $x_2 = \dfrac{m}{p_2} - \dfrac{p_1}{p_2} * x_1$
- If x_1 is 0, than we have the amount of $x_2 = \dfrac{m}{p_2}$

  => Every point on or under the blue line in the figure is a possible consumption combination of good 1 and 2.
- If one consumer don't want to consume good 1, than he/she can consume m/p_2 units of good 2.
- The slope of the blue curve is m = - p_1 / p_2.

  → This relation shows how much of good 1 the consumer has to give up to get one more unit of good 2 and vice versa.

  => Willingness to trade, opportunity costs
- **Two possible events having an impact on the consumption possibility frontier.**
  - Increase / decrease in income: Curve will shift to the right / left, slope won't change.
  - Increase / decrease in the price of one good: The intersect of the curve and the related good-axis will be shorten / extended, so the slope will increase / decrease too.

- **Preferences.**
  - **Principle of Rationality**: A decision-maker will always choose the best possible alternative.
  - In reality mistakes will occur because no decision-maker can foresee every possible consequence of his/her decision.

    → Assumption that decision-makers in here will always choose the best alternative.
  - **New notation is introduced.**
    - If the consumer prefers x strictly over y => x > y
    - If the consumer like x better or equal than y => x ≥ y
    - If the consumer doesn't care about having x or y => x ~ y

      => This concept is only ordinal, it tells about what is preferred, not by how much.
  - **Assumptions about preferences.**
    - **(1) Completeness**   Either x > y or y > x has to be right.
    - You can always give an answer to the question about preferences.
    - **(2) Reflexivity**   x ≥ x   no 'holes' in the preference relations should occur.
    - **(3) Transitivity**   x > y and y > z   than   x > z   → consistency
    - **(4) Non-Satiation // Monotonicity**   x ≥ y if x contains a few units more than y
      - x > y if x contains more units than y   → "More is better than less"
    - **(5) Strict Convexity**   t * x + (1 – t) * y > x   if t is between 0 and 1
      - Averages are preferred over extremes.
      - X = (1,4)   Y = (5, 2)   t = ½   → Z = (3,3)   z > x, y because z is the average.

- **Indifference curves** shows all possible, maximum consumption combinations (3,3 is possible, but 4,4 too, so only 4,4 will be on the curve; 3,3 below it).
- Strict convexity tells us that the middle of this curve is preferred but later we will combine the budget constraint with the preferences to calculated / find out the best alternative to choose.

- **Two extreme cases of indifference curves.**
  - **(1) Substitutes.**
    - Consumer do not care about whether to have

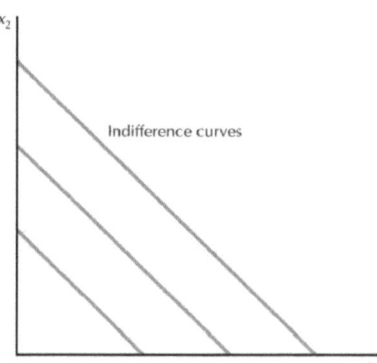

6

good one or good two.
- The only thing that matters is the amount.
- On each curve the amount of good one and two is the same, only the combination of both changed.
- The willingness to trade is exactly one (one unit of good one with one unit of good two and vice versa), but is wished to be higher.
- **Marginal rate of substitution** equals the exchange rate.
  - Find for non-linear indifference curves, is the slope of the tangent in one specific point (first derivation of indifference curve).
  - Shows the "opportunity costs" for trading, how much of good one is likely to be traded for one unit of good two.
- **(2) Perfect complements.**
- Only each new pair will increase the well-being of the consumer.
- If the consumer gets only one unit of good one and no additional unit of good two, the consumer is not better off.
- Only the total amount of pairs increases the well-being of the consumer increases and reached a higher level (= curve in the figure).

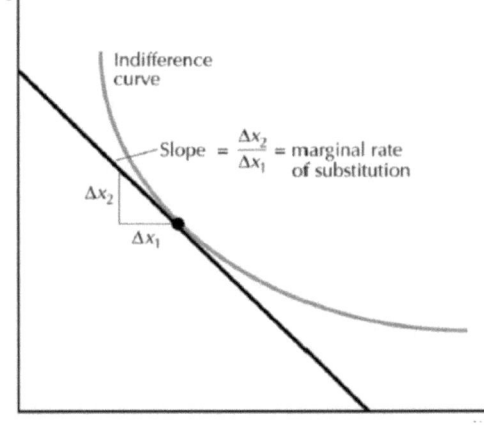

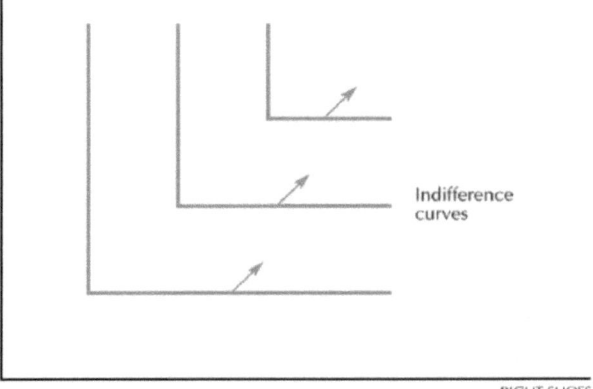

- **Looking back to strict convexity and the indifference curves.**
- The points x and y have their own indifference curves depending on which good is preferred over the other.
- If calculating the average z than this point has a specific, new indifference curve which is higher than the two of x and y.
- Furthermore, if you choose two extreme points you can examine the willingness to trade because it changes depending on the circumstances.
- If the consumer has a lot of good 1, he/she is

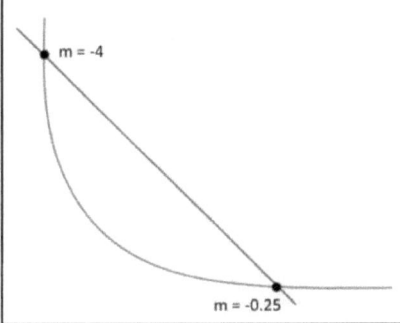

7

willing to change more of them to receive one unit of good two than if he/she has more of good two.
- Slope of -4 means to give up four units of good two to get one new of good one.
- Slope of -0.25 means to give up -0.25 units of good one to get 1 new unit of good two.

- Consumption possibility frontier reveals the possibility to trade.
- Indifference curves reveal the willingness to trade
  => Connection of both allows to determine the best alternative to choose.

Sessions Three and Four: Utility, Demand and Choice.

- **The Utility Function.**
  - A utility function must show the preferences in the right way.
    - $x > y$ should be the same like $u(x) > u(y)$ and vice versa.
    - $x \sim y$ should be the same like $u(x) = u(y)$.
  - To check a function, e.g. $u(x, y) = x * y$ insert some surveyed preferences.
    $\rightarrow$ It reveals the hierarchy, the rang of each consumption bundle.
  - Indifference curves are the level curves of the utility function.
  - But there are several possibilities to reveal the hierarchy of preferences.
  - Choosing every other function revealing those order is acceptable,

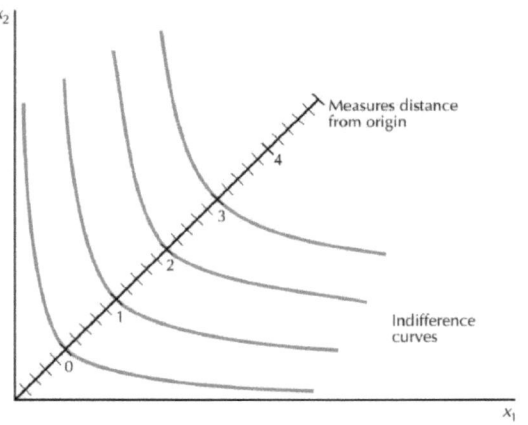

  the absolute value doesn't matters, but the marginal utility change is relevant.
    $\rightarrow$ Invariance to positive transformation.
    => **Monotonic transformation.**
  - For every $v(x, y)$ being $v(x, y) = f(u(x, y))$ if f is strictly increasing the order is right.
    $\rightarrow$ Only the labels of utility altering.

- **Marginal Utility.**
  - Marginal utility for good one is always positive
    $$\frac{\Delta u(x, y)}{\Delta x} > 0$$
  - $u(x, y) = x^{0.5} * y^{0.5}$ marginal utility $\rightarrow u_x(x, y) = 0.5 * x^{-0.5} * y^{-0.5} = \sqrt{x}$ over $2 * \sqrt{y} > 0$
  - Marginal utility is positive for every additional good x or y, but the marginal utility is decreasing.
  - Proved by the second derivative

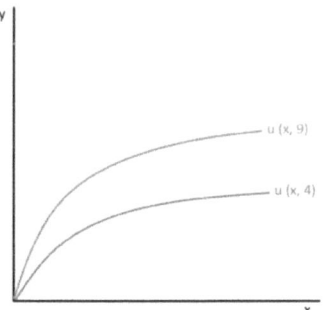

    $$u_{x,x}(x, y) = -\frac{1}{4} * x^{-\frac{3}{2}} * \sqrt{y} < 0$$

    => Increasing amount of x is better, utility is positive, but the marginal utility is decreasing.
    $\rightarrow$ First law of Gossen.

8

- **Cross-partial derivative**: Holding y constant and giving it a special number, e.g. 4 or 9.
- $u(x, y) = x^{0.5} * y^{0.5}$ $u(x, 4) = 2 * \sqrt{x}$ $u(x, 9) = 3 * \sqrt{x}$
  => If I have another unit of y, and than getting another unit of x, the marginal utility of this x is higher than without receiving y before.

- **Combination of Marginal Utility and Marginal Rate of Substitution.**
  - **Graphical approach.**
    - Marginal utility will also change in case of monotonic transformation, but the ratio of both marginal utilities is meaningful.
      - The utility increase in consumption of an additional good one should be as high as the decrease in consumption of good two.

$$\Delta U_{good1} + \Delta U_{good2} = 0 \quad MU_1 * \Delta x + MU_2 * \Delta y = 0 \quad equivalent\ to. \quad MRS = \frac{\Delta y}{\Delta x} = -\frac{MU_1}{MU_2}$$

  => MRS is equal to ratio of the marginal utilities with a minus sign.
  - **Mathematical formulation.**
    - MRS is just the slope of the indifference curve, which reveals the quantity of y as a function of x and v.v..
      - Taken out of the indifference curve: $y = f(x)$ $x = f(y)$
    - Define one generic indifference curve: $u(x, y) = c$
    - Remember the definition of indifference curves: Every consumption bundle with the same amount of utility (in this case: utility of c).
    - This is an implicit curve, because we have the result given, but not the x and y.
    - Chain rule (train of thought from above): Displaying y as a function of x.
      - $u(x, y(x)) = c \quad \rightarrow \quad u_x(x, y(x)) + u_y(x, y(x)) * y' = 0$
    - $MRS = slope\ of\ the\ IC = f'(x) \quad = \quad \dfrac{\Delta x}{\Delta y} \quad = \quad \dfrac{u_x(x, y)}{u_y(x, y)} \quad = \quad -\dfrac{MU_y}{MU_x}$
      - If I give up one unit of x, than I'm worse off by $u_x(x, y)$; to be better off divide this marginal utility by the marginal utility of good y to reveal how much units of y I need to receive at least to be compensated for this lack of one good x → Willingness to trade.
    - Example in numbers.
    - $u(x, y) = x * y$ $P(2, 5)$ $Q(6, 6)$
    - MRS (2,5) = -2,5   Can lose up to 2.5 marginal utility of x to increase marginal utility for y only for one.
    - MRS (6,6) = -1

- **Types of utility functions.**
  - Cobb-Douglas: $u(x, y) = x^a * y^b$ where a, b > 0
  - Perfect complements: $u(x, y) = min\ \{a*x, b*y\}$ where a, b > 0
  - Perfect substitutes: $u(x, y) = a*x + b*y$ where a, b > 0
  - Quasi-linear: $u(x, y) = f(x) + y$ (y is linear, f(x) close to, so quasi-linear).
  - Constant elasticity of substitution: will not be handled in this course.

- **Rational Choice (what to choose).**
  - Putting budget line and indifference curves together in one framework.
  - Choose a bundle (x*, y*) which provides together the highest utility among affordable bundles.
  - Mathematical formalization: max u (x, y) with the constraint of $p_1 * x + p_2 * y \le m$.

- Combine the budget line (gray) with the indifference curve (red).
- Point P (intersect with the budget line) can't be the optimal point because if I give away two units of y, I claim for one good of x, but can receive two.
  → I'm better off than before.
- Marginal rate of substitution in P is lower than the slope of the budged line.
  - Internal exchange rate (MRS) is smaller than the market exchange rate, therefore trading will make better off.
- The same thing is to be observed at Point Q, so the optimal choice has to be in between P and Q.

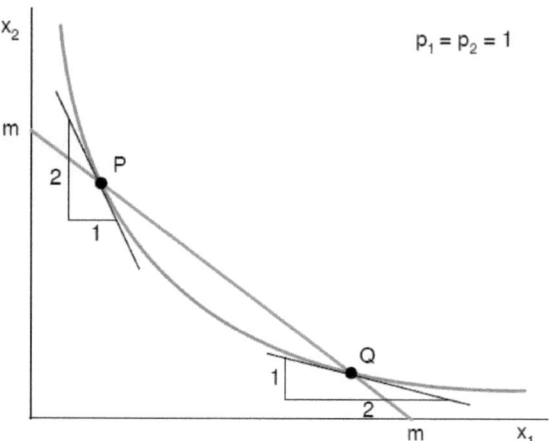

=> Best consumption bundle is where the internal exchange rate equals the market exchange rate.
  → Getting to the highest indifference curve we can afford with out budget.
- We can state **two conditions of optimal choice**.
  - (1) Internal exchange rate must be equal to the market exchange rate.
  - (2) All your budget has to be spend because every euro spent will make you better off.
- **Graphical solution**: The optimal choice is the point, where the highest possible indifference curve tangents the budget line.
- Rate of willingness to trade equals the rate of possibility to trade.

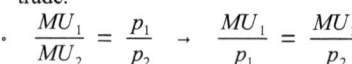
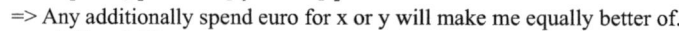

- $$\frac{MU_1}{MU_2} = \frac{p_1}{p_2} \quad \rightarrow \quad \frac{MU_1}{p_1} = \frac{MU_2}{p_2}$$

=> Any additionally spend euro for x or y will make me equally better of.

- If $\frac{MU_x}{p_x} > \frac{MU_y}{p_y}$ than we prefer x over y, our marginal utility for every euro spend on good x is higher than the marginal utility from every euro spend on good y.

- **Mathematical solution.**
  - Cover the same problem as before with mathematical formalization.

10

- Solve the constrained maximization problem by setting up the Lagrangian.
- Ł = u (x, y) – λ * (p₁*x + p₂*y – m)

  $Ł = u (x, y) - \lambda * (p_1*x + p_2*y - m)$
- λ ≥ 0, λ * (p₁*x + p₂*y – m) = 0

  $\lambda \geq 0, \; \lambda * (p_1*x + p_2*y - m) = 0$
  - Because of our further assumptions, we can identify λ.
    - It can't be 0 because than the marginal utility at this point has to be zero and neither the MU of x nor y will ever be 0 (assumption of monocity).
    - Can't be negative because there is always a benefit from consuming or having one good more.
    → The term (p₁*x + p₂*y – m) has to be 0.
    → Only if we spend all our budget, we will be best-off; if I'm always better off if receiving another unit, I will spend all my money on getting as much I can afford.

- **Optimal Choice for perfect substitutes.**
  - For perfect substitutes the rule $\dfrac{MU_1}{p_1} = \dfrac{MU_2}{p_2}$ won't be fulfilled.
  - You only care about the total amount to be better off, so you prefer buying the cheaper one.
    - If the prices are the same, than this model can't tell anything about the consumption bundle.
  - Slope of the indifference curve is always -1 (for perfect substitutes).
  - If slope of the budged line is $\dfrac{p_x}{p_y} < -1$ so prefer buying x over y
    → Corner solution, best choice is to buy only x and no y
    - Demand function for x: x* = m over p₁
    - Demand function for y: y* = 0
  - If the price for y changes, the intersect with the y-axis will change.
    => Therefore utility function looks like u (x, y) = p₁ * x + p₂ * y.

- **Optimal choice for perfect complements.**
  - The best choice is the bundle which provides the highest amount of pairs.
  - If having more x than y, this solution is inefficient because you could offer the same level of well-being with less money.
  - The highest complement indifference curve tangenting the budged line is the optimal choice.
  - U (x, y) = min {x, y} with the constraint that x = y
    - *Demand function*: $x_* = y_* = \dfrac{m}{p_1* \, p_2}$

- **Role of the demand curve in thinking about optimal choice.**
  - x* is a function of p₁, p₂ and m, so → x* (p₁, p₂, m).
  - Effects of changes of price for the own good, price for the other good, and income.

	≤ 0 (negative) quantity decrease	≥ 0 (positive) quantity increase
Δx over Δp₁ price increases	**Ordinary good**	**Giffen good**
Δx over Δm income increases	**Inferior good**	**Normal good**
Δx over Δp₂ price for the other good increases	**Complements**	**Substitutes**

- **Looking in detail on Δp₁.**

11

- The initial price p' determines the slope of the budget line and the optimal choice.
- If p' increases to p" the quantity demanded decreases, the budget line becomes steeper, but the starting point (intersect with the y-axis) remains the same.
- If the price for y is increasing, the intersect with the y-axis decreases and the slope becomes flatter.
- With the information of p_1' and p_1" as well as the related quantity demanded, we can create the demand function.
  - If price for good two increases, the quantity demanded decreases at the same price of good one. → Shift in the demand curve to the left, so these two goods were complements.
- **Price-Offer-Curve**: Curve arising when connecting the single optimal choices points for every price 1.

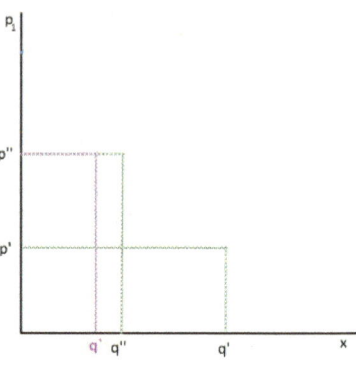

- **Substitution Effect and Income Effect.**
  - The total quantity effect of one good is determined by income effect and substitution effect.
    - **Substitution effect** shows how much consumers substitute away from more expensive goods.
    - **Income effect** shows the purchasing price of consumer (increases or decreases with lower / higher prices).
    => Every time the price changes, the both effects occur simultaneously.
  - To isolate the substitution effect, we have the price change to the old consumption bundle the consumer could afford with the new prices.

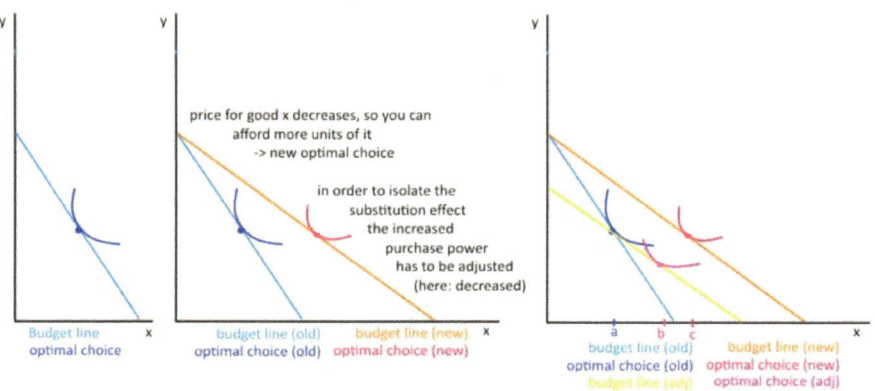

- The quantity effect we can observe is the increase from a → c (total effect).
- Now we have to distinguish how great the income effect and substitution effect are.
  - *Substitution effect*: Because of our adjustment of the purchasing power, we can observe the isolated substitution effect which is a → b.
  - *Income effect*: We undo our adjustment starting from b and going to c.
- **General.**
  - The substitution effect is always negative because price increase leads to decrease in quantity and vice versa.
  - Income effect can be either positive (normal goods) or negative (inferior goods).
- **Mathematical formalization.**
  - Slutsky demand
$$x_1^s = x_1(p_1, p_2, p_1 \overline{x}_1 + p_2 \overline{x}_2)$$

12

- $\bar{x}_1$ = old amount of x_1
- Answers the question about what is the new demand x^s_1 if I have the new prices and want to afford the old amount of goods.

$$\underbrace{\frac{\partial x_1(p_1, p_2, \overline{m})}{\partial p_1}}_{\text{Total effect}} = \underbrace{\frac{\partial x^s_1}{\partial p_1}}_{\text{Substitution effect}} - \underbrace{\frac{\partial x_1(p_1, p_2, \overline{m})}{\partial m} \bar{x}_1}_{\text{Income effect}}$$

- **Explanation.**
  - In the example (graphs) above we know that the substitution effect is negative. We observe that the total effect as well as the others go into the same direction. Because of the minus sign before the income effect term in the equation above, the income effect has to be positive to produce a negative total effect.
  - In the example above we have an **ordinary good** (price decreases, quantity demanded increases) and an **normal good** (income increases, quantity demanded increases).
  - Case of **inferior good**: substitution effect still is negative (price decreases, quantity demanded increases), income effect is negative too (income increases, quantity demanded decreases).
    → If total effect is positive or negative depends on SE < IE or SE > IE.
  - For Giffen goods the substitution effect is positive (price increases, quantity demanded too).

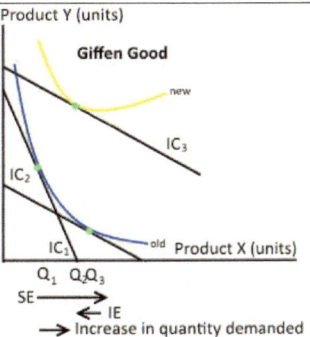

- **Price changes in extreme cases.**
  - **(1) Perfect complements.**
    - The substitution effect is zero because you can't substitute perfect complements.
    - Also because the adjusted budget line will always have the same optimal choice than the old budget line.
    => Even though the price of only one good is decreased we can now afford more pairs to be better-off than before.
  - **(2) Perfect substitutes.**
    - There is no income effect because only corner solutions are the best.
      - For every corner solution the adjusted budget line equals the new one.

13

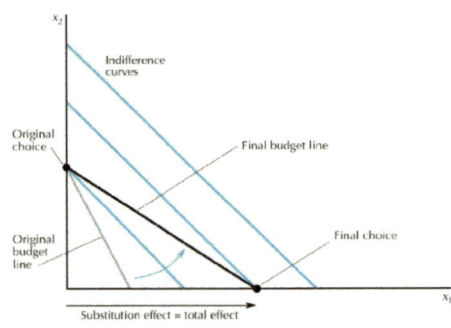

Substitution effect = total effect

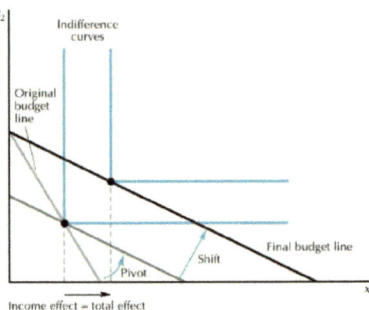

Income effect = total effect

- **(3) Quasi-linear preferences.**
  - The choice of good one is independent of income, but then the amount of good two that can be offered is limited to the remaining budget.
  - In this case there is no income effect because price of good one only affects good two.

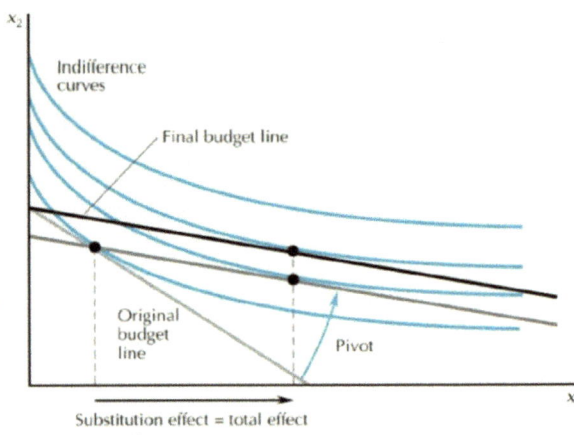

Substitution effect = total effect

- **Experiment to determine Giffen behavior.**
  - The normal diet is based on a consumption bundle of basic food and fancy food.
  - Of course all people want to eat only fancy food, but they need basic food to keep them over the level of subsistence.
  - Therefore we have to distinguish three kinds of zones important for the preferences.
    - **Black line**: Subsistence level, minimum diet you need to survive.
    - **Red zone**: You can't afford enough to eat, so you only care about the amount of food, not which kind this is → behavior like for perfect substitutes.

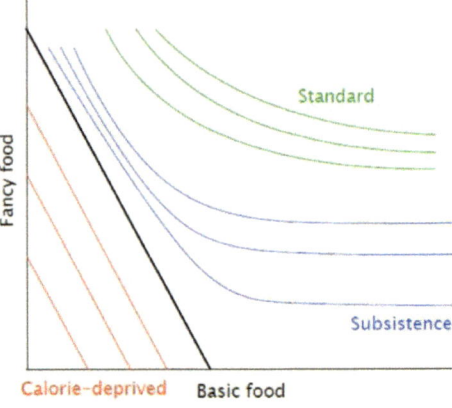

- **Green zone**: You will never have to fear starvation, so the indifference curves are normal.
- **Blue zone**: Transition between normal and perfect substitutes behavior, the closer you get to the subsistence level, the more you behave like perfect substitutes; the wider away you are from this, the more you behave like normal.
  => Quasi-linear function.

- Three people living in different zones have different budget lines.
- If the price for basic food increases, the budget lines will become steeper.
- You can observe different behavior.
  - The corner solution of perfect substitutes has to decrease its total consumption because with the old income less basic food is affordable.
  - The standard zone decreases the quantity demanded of basic food.
  - The middle zone fears to starve and increases its consumption of basic food even though the prices has increased.
    - If less purchasing power to buy food, than spend more money on basic food and less on fancy food to ensure living above the level of subsistence.

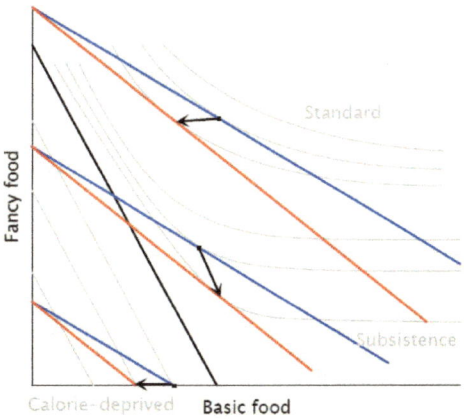

- **Four conditions Giffen behavior was observed.**
- (1) Households face subsistence nutrition concerns.
- (2) Households consume simple diet, consumption bundle of basic and fancy food.
- (3) Basic food is cheapest source of calories available.
- (4) Households will never only consume basic food (except you face starvation).

Lectures 6 and 7: Consumer's surplus, market demand and equilibrium.

- **Measuring utility in money.**
- This is equal to the consumer's surplus.
- Reservation price r_1: highest price to pay to consume the first unit of one good.
- Reservation price r_2: highest price to pay to consume the second unit of one good.
  => Equal to the marginal utility.
- Quasi-linear function: $u(x, y) = f(x) + y$
  - Consumption of good x is not depending on budget, the rest of the budget is spent on good y.
  - $p_1 * x + p_2 * y = m \quad \rightarrow \quad y = m - p_1 * x$
- $u(x, y) = f(x) + m - p_1 * x$
  - How much else I can consume beside my actual consumption of x.
- **Calculation of reservation price.**
  - In which case it doesn't matter if you buy or not → this is your highest reservation price.
  - Buy nothing: $u(0) = f(0) + m$
  - Buy one unit: $u(1) = f(1) + m - r_1 * 1 \quad$ (price = r_1)
  - For which $r_1 \ u(0) = u(1)$ holds?
    - This will be the reservation price because I'm exactly indifferent whether to buy or not.
    - $r_1 = f(1) - f(0)$
      - Marginal utility of consuming the first unit of good one.
  - Reservation price for the consumption of another good.
    - $u(1) = f(1) + m - r_2 * 1$
    - $u(2) = f(2) + m - r_2 * 2$
    - $u(1) = u(2) \quad\quad\quad r_2 = f(2) - f(1)$
      - marginal utility of consuming the second unit of good one.

15

- **Consumer's surplus.**
  - Visual display of all reservation prices and the marginal utility received from consuming the goods → *Gross surplus*.
  - *Net surplus*: Price limits the marginal utility of consumption, therefore you only want to buy the much units your reservation price is higher or equal the market price to receive a surplus.

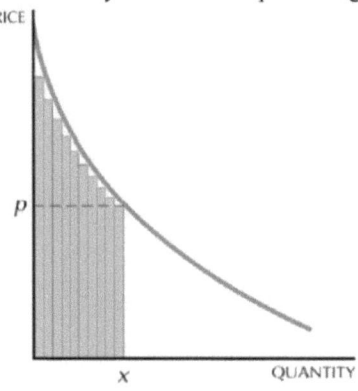 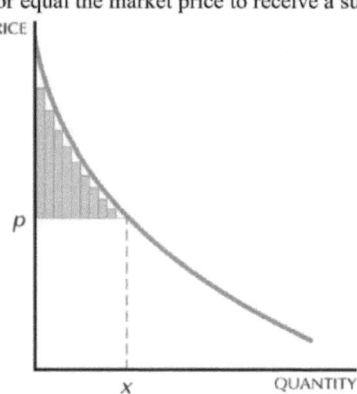

A Approximation to gross surplus   **B** Approximation to net surplus

- Market demand is the approximation of all individual reservation prices.
- The maximum market entrance price you are willing to pay to go to market is equal or less the utility you gain from the purchase of goods.
- **A caveat.**
  - Demand function is not the same as the reservation price function because of the income effect.
  - In all further cases the reservation price function is equal to the demand function, the income effect is neglected.
- **Effect of a price change.**
  - Changes in price will reduce / increase the consumer's surplus.
  - If price falls from p" to p', than the consumer surplus is increased by the areas of R and T as well as vice versa.

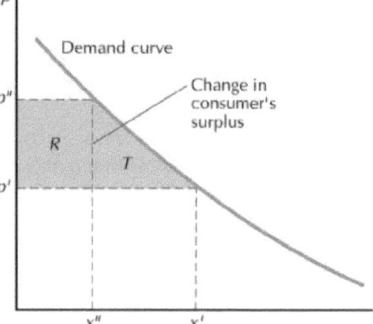

- **Producer's surplus.**
  - Not quite equal to profits.
  - Marginal costs of production.
  - Areas R + T = by how much I'm worse off / better-off if price decreases / increases.

- **Price Elasticity of Demand.**
  - **(1) Midpoint Method // Arc Elasticity of Demand.**
    - Calculating the elasticity between two different points on the demand curve.
    - Problem is the order of the two points (from A to B is differs from B to A).
    - Dividing the difference of A and B with the midpoint of them (A+B) / 2 will ensure the same results only with changing signs.

- *Price elastaicity of demand* $= \dfrac{\dfrac{Q_2 - Q_1}{(Q_2 + Q_1)/2}}{\dfrac{P_2 - P_1}{(P_2 + P_1)/2}}$ → $\varepsilon = D'(p) * \dfrac{p}{D(p)}$ First derivative of demand function to p * q

- **(2) Point Elasticity of Demand.**
  - Price elasticity of demand for one special point in the curve.
  - *Price elasticity of demand* $= \dfrac{P}{x} * \dfrac{Delta\ x}{Delta\ P}$
- Unit-elastic functions: $\varepsilon = 1$
- Inelastic functions: $\varepsilon > -1$
- Elastic functions: $\varepsilon < -1$
  → The higher, the stronger the reaction on price changes.
- Sugar is very small amount of our budget, so we don't care about the price, just drive to the supermarket and buy it if we need it.
- In the long-term things are more elastic than in the short-run.

- **Elasticity and revenue.**
  - To increase the revenue the quantity must be increased, but this is only possible by decreasing the price.
  - Revenue as function of p can be expressed as price * quantity supplied as $R(p) = p \cdot q(p)$ function of p.
  - To study the changes in revenue we have to calculate the first derivative.
    $R'(p) = q(p)(1 + \varepsilon)$
  - If the function is inelastic, ε is greater than -1 so the term is positive and the revenue can be increased with higher price.
  - If the function is elastic, ε is smaller than -1 so the term is negative and the revenue decreases.
    → If your are price setter, set the price above the inelastic interval and below the elastic one because then you receive the greatest revenue.
  - If $\varepsilon = -1$, than the gain from price increase equals the loss from quantity decrease.
  - This is also the maximum of the demand function → Revenue maximized.

- **Linear Demand.**
  - Suppose $q(p) = a - b * p$
  - In each point on the curve the elasticity is different.
  - Calculate the points when elasticity should be -1 by inserting -1 in the ε equation.
  - $p = \dfrac{a}{2b}$ $q = \dfrac{a}{2}$

- **Isoelastic Demand.**
  - In each point of the curve, the elasticity is the same.

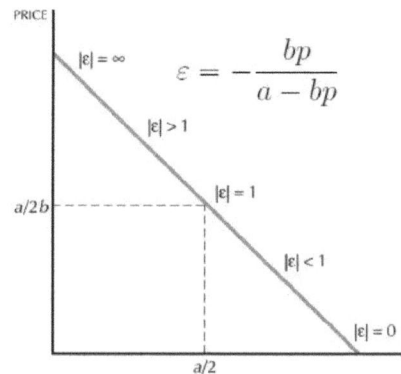

17

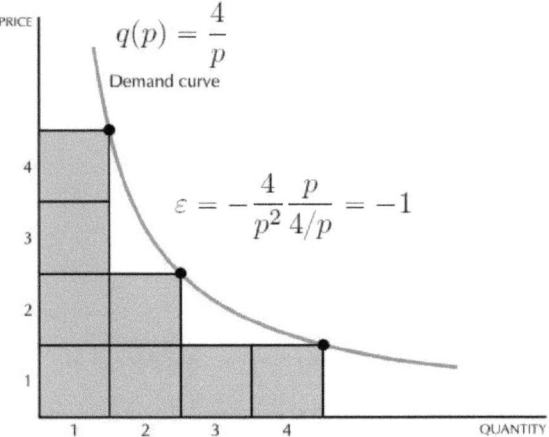

PRICE

$$q(p) = \frac{4}{p}$$

Demand curve

$$\varepsilon = -\frac{4}{p^2}\frac{p}{4/p} = -1$$

QUANTITY

- The flatter the curve, the longer the consideration.
- In the long run, the supply is fully elastic.

- **Equilibrium and Welfare.**
  - D (p*) = S (p*)   Intersection of the demand and the supply curve.
  - P* means that plans of consumers meet plans of producers.
  - Welfare is the sum of consumers surplus and producers surplus.
    → A competitive market maximizes the total welfare / the gains of exchange.
  - This model will be the benchmark, all future models will be compared to this utopia.

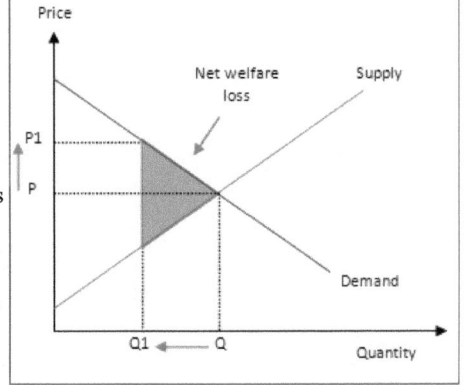

- $Consumers'\,surplus \ = \ \int_{0}^{Q} D(Q)\,dQ \ - \ P^{optimum} * Q^{optimum}$

- $Producers'\,surplus \ = \ p^{optimum} * q^{optimum} \ - \ \int_{0}^{Q} S(Q)\,dQ$

- **Taxation (one policy measure).**
  - **Sin taxes**: Taxes on goods being harmful for a market economy (alcohol, tobacco).
  - P* is the optimal price of the market, but a tax will influence this.
    - P_s is the price the producers receive; P_d the price the consumers have to pay.
    - $P_s = P_d - t$ <=> $P_d = P_s + t$
      => It doesn't matter who has to pay the tax legally because the result will be the same.
  - If the consumers are taxed, the demand decreases (shift downwards); the new equilibrium point will reveal P_s the price the producers will receive.
  - If the producers are taxed, the supply decreases (shift upwards); the new equilibrium will

18

reveal P_d the price the consumers have to pay.
=> Difference in the welfare which side of the market is taxed.

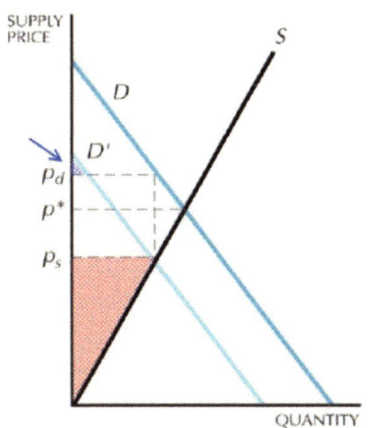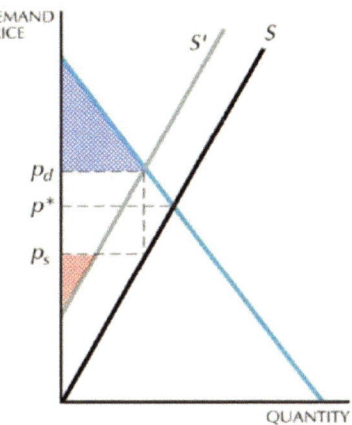

- Question about **which side has to pay which percentage of the tax**? (fixed tax, no percentage one).
  - Difference of P_d and p^* seems to be smaller than P_s and p^*.
    → Tax burden depends on elasticity of both market sides.

$$\frac{P_d - p_* \cdot}{t} = \frac{P_d - p_* \cdot}{P_d - p_* \cdot + p_* \cdot - P_s}$$

$$\varepsilon \approx \frac{\frac{\Delta q}{q}}{\frac{p_d - p^*}{p}} \quad \eta \approx \frac{\frac{\Delta q}{q}}{\frac{p_s - p^*}{p}} \quad = \quad \frac{\frac{\Delta q}{q} \cdot \frac{\varepsilon}{p}}{p_d - p^* + p_s - p^*}$$

- **Tax incidence** $= \dfrac{\eta}{\eta + |\varepsilon|}$
  - The more elastic the demand curve, the less the consumers have to pay.
  - If η decreases (inelastic supply), producers tax burden will increase.
    => Formula answers the question how much of the tax has to be paid by the consumer.
- **Numerical example.**
  - Elasticity of demand equals -0.5, elasticity of supply equals 5
  - Tax incidence reveals that around 91% of the tax has to be paid by the consumer.
    - *Explanation*: The demand curve is rather inelastic, so consumers have less alternatives to buy; therefore this side has to carry nearly the whole tax burden. Furthermore producers can easily leave the market (use employees, machinery and raw material to produce other goods).
  - In the long-term: All taxes will be passed on the consumer.
  - With this model we can calculate if the government intentions are likely to be fulfilled or not.
    - **Sugar Tax**: Government wants the citizen to consume less sugar drinks because of health problems. Taxation of sugar should be carried by the producers. If we have the intended tax rate and the elasticity of demand, we can calculate the elasticity of supply (not known because companies' secret) and assess whether this is likely the case or not.
- **Criticism of this model (formula).**
  - (1) We are using old data and compare it with new data. The elasticity before the tax is used to

19

reveal the elasticity after the tax is introduced.
- (2) Assumption that the market is completely competitive is not correct. Some companies have market power and make (high) profits. A tax will reduce the profits, but not terminate them, so there is no incentive to reduce production for the suppliers.
- Better way to fulfill government intentions is setting up special rules to decrease the demand (restrictions to make the goods less available).

- **Extreme cases – tax incidence.**
  - **Fully elastic supply**: Tax has to be completely paid by consumers.
  - **Fully inelastic supply**: Tax has to be completely paid by producers.
  - The more inelastic the market side is, the more taxes this market side has to pay.

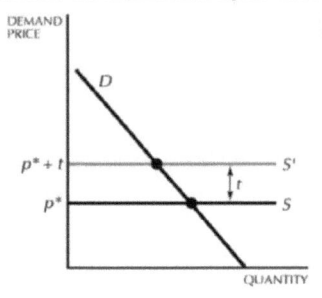 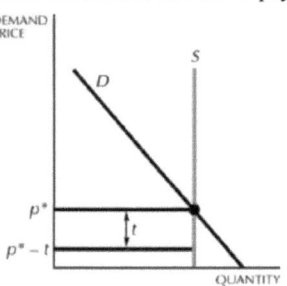

- **Welfare analysis of taxes.**
  - Taxes do not necessarily require shifts in the demand / supply.
  - The new market price related to the tax reduces the total welfare by the areas of B and D.
    → Dead-weight losses.
  - The areas A and C are no losses, they represent a redistribution from consumers and producers surplus to the government.
    => The more elastic the both curves are, the greater the dead-weight loss will be.

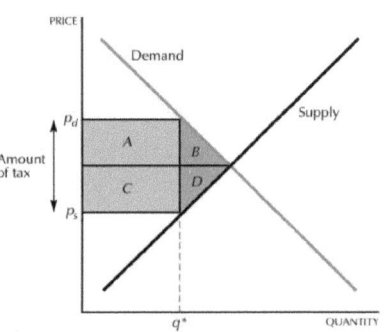

- **Introduction of a price ceiling.**
  - Producers surplus decreases from BED to D.
  - Total welfare decreases.
  - Consumers surplus changes, but we can't determine how.
  - Because of the artificial shortage (excess demand) the market doesn't allocate the goods any longer.

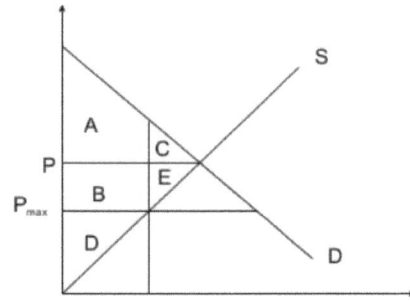

Lectures 8 & 9: Technology, profit maximization and cost minimization.

- **Theory of the firm.**
  - Assumption: Firm simply converts input into output.
  - Input creates costs: Labor (wages), capital (interest rate), land (lease), licenses (licensing fee).
  - Formalize the whole production process in one production function
    => y = f (x) (x = Input; y = Output).
- **Production set.**
  - The amount of output I can produce with a given amount of input.
  - Always produce at the production line because every point below is inefficient.
  - I can produce a point below the production line with less input or with the same input I could produce more.
- **Marginal product.**
  - f' (x) = marginal product.
  - Same idea as in the marginal rate of utility; marginal change of output if input is increased.
  - All production functions will decrease the ratio between input and output after reaching a certain point (remember the first law of Gossen).

- **Isoquants.**
  - Same idea as indifference curves; all combinations of input needed to produce the same quantity of outputs.
  - Two input factors x and y, we can use them to produce a certain output.
  - The level of isoquant has to be the same to be equally of.
  - The more good x I have the more output I can produce, x and y are not perfect complements.

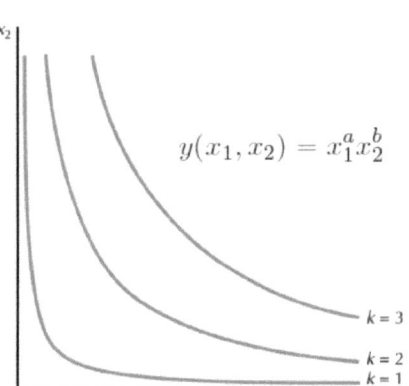

$$y(x_1, x_2) = x_1^a x_2^b$$

- **Extreme cases of Isoquants.**
  - Fixed proportions // "Leontieff" (perfect complements).
    - I have a fixed need of good x and good y to produce one unit of output.
  - Only be able to increase output if the bundle of x and y is increasing, increase in x alone won't make me better off.
  - Perfect substitutes.
    - I can substitute input factor x with y, so the optimal choice is always a corner solution.

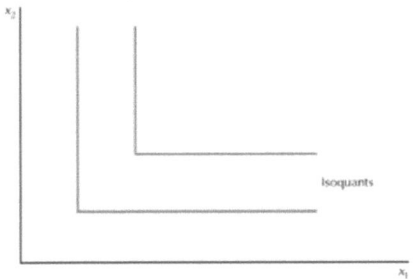

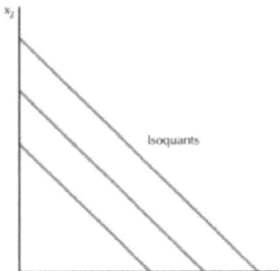

21

- **Technical rate of substitution TRS.**
  - Suppose we have three different machinery subject to capital and labor.
  - An expensive machine needs less workers and vice versa.
  - Three different machines have all L-formed isoquants (fixed proportions), but the mixture of the quantity of machines can be changes (not only one machine each, increase the amount).
  => Receiving the "normal" isoquants.
  - TRS gives the ratio revealing how much of input factor x has to be given up in order to receive one more unit of y.

$$f(x_1, x_2) = k$$

$$\frac{dx_2}{dx_1} = -\frac{\partial f(x_1, x_2)/\partial x_1}{\partial f(x_1, x_2)/\partial x_2}$$

$$= -\frac{\text{Marginal product of 1}}{\text{Marginal product of 2}}$$

- **Returns to scale (Economies of Scale).**
  - Question is: How much my output changes if I double/triple etc. all input factors.
  - Three different cases.
    - **Constant** returns to scale: $f(t*x, t*y) = t * f(x, y)$.
    - If I double all input factors, the output will be doubled too.
    - **Increasing** returns to scale: $f(t*x, t*y) > t * f(x, y)$.
    - If I double all input factors, the output will increase by more than the double quantity.
    - **Decreasing** returns to scale: $f(t*x, t*y) < t * f(x, y)$.
    - If I double all input factors, the output will increase by less than the double quantity.
  - Theoretical Example.
    - Degree of homogeneity = a + b

$$f(x_1, x_2) = x_1^a x_2^b$$

$$f(tx_1, tx_2) = (tx_1)^a (tx_2)^b$$
$$= t^a t^b x_1^a x_2^b$$
$$= t^{a+b} f(x_1, x_2)$$

	Returns to scale
$a + b = 1$	constant
$a + b > 1$	increasing
$a + b < 1$	decreasing

- **Output elasticizes.**

$$y = f(x, y) = x^a * y^b$$

$$\text{output elasticity } f_x = \frac{x}{f(x, y)} = a * x^{a-1} * y^b * \frac{x}{x^a * y^b} = a$$

=> The exponent tells me the elasticity of this good.
  - Special feature of Cobb-Douglas functions:
    Returns to scale = sum of elasticizes (a + b).

- **Empirics on returns to scale.**
  - Calculated by Hsieh in 1995, reveals the returns to scale on the basis of a Cobb-Douglas function with the two input factors capital and labor.
  - Shows the problems of our simplified theory of the firm.
    - The norm should be constant returns to scale because nothing restricts the input factors capital and labor.
    → Scarcity is neglected, volatility of markets

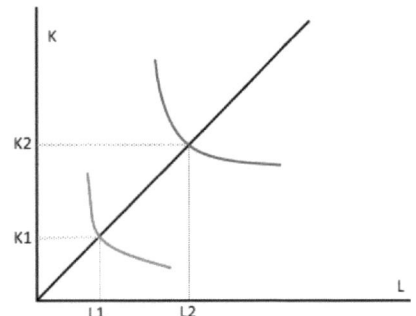

22

and everything else.

- **Profit maximization.**
  - Depends on demand and elasticity.
  - Depends on market structure (which determines how much of the whole demand comes to one single company).
  - Profit is the sum of all revenue minus the sum of all costs.
    - There are actually two ways to compute the costs, the accounting method and the real cost method (including opportunity costs).
      => From now on, only the real costs are considered.
  - Distinction of short-run and long-run maximization because in the long-run all input factors are variable, in the short-run at least one is fixed.
  - **Consider the long-run first.**

$$\max_{K,L} \pi = pf(K, L) - rK - wL$$

  - Optimization of the equation above reveals the value of the additional production of one new worker $\pi_L(K, L) = p * MP_L = w$
    => Marginal revenue product.
  - Equilibrium of the market means marginal revenue product = marginal costs.
    - If mrp is greater than mc, than hiring additional workers will increase revenue and vice versa.
  - $MP_L = w/P$ How much of the product I can afford if I work one hour for the company.
    → Wage the worker earns in real terms.
  - $w = MP_L * p$ and $r = MP_K * p$ demand functions of labor and capital.
- **Now consider the short-run.**
  - At least one input factor is fixed, lets take labor for fixed.
  - Maximization of this function will lead us to the same result than mentioned above.

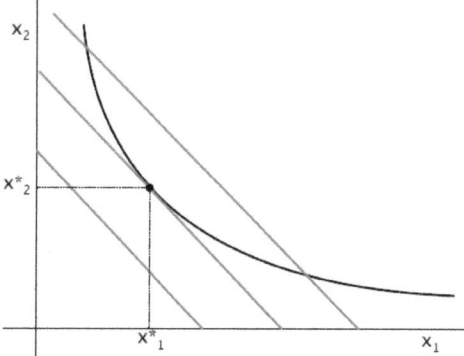

- **Cost minimization.**
  - Input factors x_1 and x_2 are processed with technology displayed by the function $y = f(x_1, x_2)$.
  - Price for x_1 is w_1, price for x_2 is w_2.
  - Solving this problem means solving $C = x_1 * w_1 + x_2 * w_2$ with the constraint of $y = f(x_1, x_2)$.
  - Cost function C will give us all combinations of input factors that have a total cost of 100.
    → Isocost line (similar idea of indifference curves).
  - Slope of the isoquant has to be the same as slope of the isocost line.
  - Conditional demand function arises.
  - $X_2^* = C/w_2 - w_1/w_2 * x_1^*$
    → Conditional because it depends on what I want to produce.
  - $C(y) = w_1 * x_1^* + w_2 * x_2^*$ for every y the costs can be calculated.
  - $\dfrac{MP_2}{w_2} = \dfrac{MP_1}{w_1}$ Should be equal otherwise the costs could be minimized.
    - By how much does costs change if I spend one more euro on the input factor.
- **Example with the Cobb-Douglas function.**

Minimize costs of this equation

$$y = x_1^a x_2^{1-a}$$

$$\frac{a x_1^{a-1} x_2^{1-a}}{(1-a) x_1^a x_2^{-a}} = \frac{w_1}{w_2}$$

$$y = x_1^a x_2^{1-a}$$

conditional demand functions

$$x_1^*(w_1, w_2, y) = \left(\frac{a}{1-a}\right)^{1-a} \left(\frac{w_2}{w_1}\right)^{1-a} y$$

$$x_2^*(w_1, w_2, y) = \left(\frac{1-a}{a}\right)^{a} \left(\frac{w_1}{w_2}\right)^{a} y$$

$$C(w_1, w_2, y) = w_1 x_1^*(w_1, w_2, y) + w_2 x_2^*(w_1, w_2, y)$$

- **Overview of the concepts introduced in this lectures.**

Utility	Production	Mathematical concept
Marginal utility	Marginal product	Derivative
Indifference curve	Isoquant	Level curve
MRS	TRS	Slope of level curve
Budget constraint	Isocost line	
Demand function	Factor demand	Solution
Indirect utility	Cost function	Value function

- Value function: Whenever x* is calculated, plug it into the original function and receive the indirect utility or the total costs.
- Differences: Utility faces a maximization problem, production a minimization problem.

Lectures 10 and 11: Costs and Supply.

- **Cost curves.**
- The cost minimization reveals the optimal cost function.

$$C(w_1, w_2, y) = w_1 x_1^*(w_1, w_2, y) + w_2 x_2^*(w_1, w_2, y)$$

- If the value of w_1 and w_2 are fixed, the **cost function** will look like C (y).
- **Average costs** are defined as C (y) / y   and **marginal costs** as C ' (y)
- In the short-run we have fixed costs C (0) because at least one input factor is fixed.
  → In the long-run we have no fix costs because all input factors are variable.
- AC = Average Costs, AVC = Average Variable Costs, AFC = Average Fixed Costs.
- AC = AVC + AFC   (AFC converges to zero, AC will increase at a certain point).
- **Relationship between marginal and average costs.**

- Cost minimization with support of average cost curve.

- $\left(\dfrac{C(y)}{y}\right)' = \dfrac{1}{y} * \left(C'(y) - \dfrac{C(y)}{y}\right)$

- First derivative of AC provides $1/y * (MC - AC)$.
  - → Average costs are increasing if MC is greater than AC and vice versa
  - => Optimal cost combination is when AC equals MC.

- The intersect of MC and AC is the minimum point of AC curve.
- Intersect of MC and AVC is also the minimum point of the AVC curve.
- AC and AVC are converging together.
- The are below the MC function represents the variable costs.

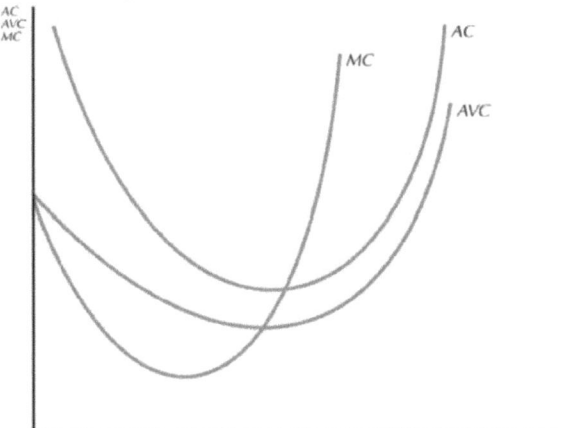

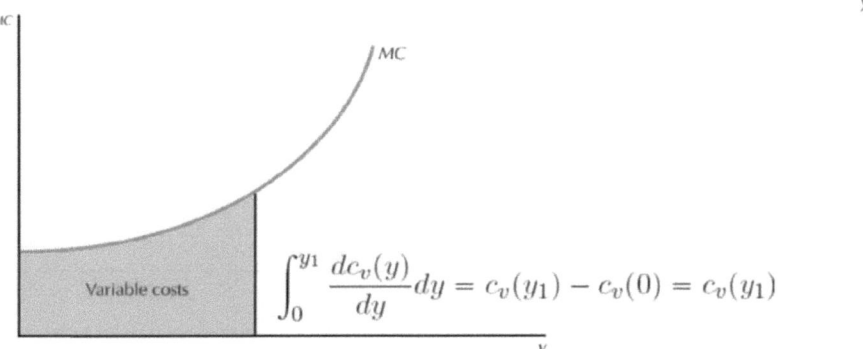

$$\int_{0}^{y_1} \frac{dc_v(y)}{dy} dy = c_v(y_1) - c_v(0) = c_v(y_1)$$

- **Elasticity of the cost function.**
- Elasticity in general: $f'(x) * (x / f(x))$
- Elasticity of cost function: $C'(y) * (y / C(y)) \rightarrow MC / AC$ = output elasticity of costs.
- **Now we can think about the returns to scale.**
  - Output elasticity of costs greater than 1 means decreasing returns to scale.
  - Output elasticity of costs smaller than 1 means increasing returns to scale.
  - Output elasticity of costs equal to 1 means constant returns to scale.
  - => If AC is decreasing, returns to scale are increasing and vice versa.

- **Market types.**
  - Two extreme cases.
    - (1) Pure competition.
      - A lot of small companies selling nearly the same products, no market power of any company,

output decisions have no impact on the price, firms as price takers, sell as much as you can at the given price.
- (2) Monopoly.
- Only one seller, free price setting process.
- In between those extremes many market types are existing, including three important ones.
  - (1) Oligopoly: Few firms, decisions are influencing the payoffs of others, incentives to create a cartel.
  - (2) Monopolistic competition: Slightly different products offered, price elasticity of the market differs from the elasticity of the firms.
  - (3) Dominant firm: One company will influence the profit of the other market participants, but not vice versa.

- **Pure Competition (the benchmark case).**
  - If p* is the market price, the demand facing one single company at a certain price p can be describes as the following:
    - If company sells above the market price p* it won't face any demand.
    - If company sells below p* it will face the whole market demand, but can't fulfill it (assumption that only small companies are existing).
  - To maximize profits the company has to sell at the market price p*.
  - The maximization of the profits curve reveals that the optimal price equals the marginal costs.
  - MC = p.
  => MC are the supply curve of the company.
  - Profit at $p^* = p^* * q - AC\ (q)$.
  - **Calculation when to leave the market and when to stay.**
  - The minimum profit of a company has to be $p^*y - c\ (y) - FC \geq -FC$
    $\rightarrow p \geq c\ (y)\ /\ y = AVC$ shut-down-condition
  - If the company's profit equals exactly the AVC, the company is indifferent whether to leave or stay in the market.
  - If the company receives more profit than the AVC it is better to stay in the market; you're still making losses, but less than if leaving the market (than you have to face the full FC).
  => Market price at least need to equal your AVC to make you stay in the market.
  - S (x) = y   x is the price, y the profit;   we know that we need at least a profit of MC
    $\rightarrow S^{-1}\ (y) = p\ (y) = x$ reveals the market price if having a given profit.

$$D^F(p) = \begin{cases} 0 \text{ if } p > p^* \\ \text{any amount if } p = p^* \\ D^M(p) \text{ if } p < p^* \end{cases}$$

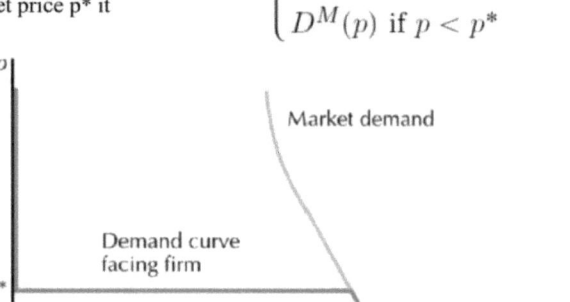

Market demand

Demand curve facing firm

$$S^{-1}(y) = p(y) = \begin{cases} MC & \text{if } p \geq \frac{c_v(y)}{y} \\ 0 & \text{if } p < \frac{c_v(y)}{y} \end{cases}$$

- **Relationship between profits and producer's surplus.**
  - Producers surplus is the area below the market price, but above the supply curve.
  - Supply curve is the MC curve, equals 0 if p is below the AVC.
    => Producer's surplus = $p^* y - c(y)$.
  - Producer's surplus = profits + FC.
  - In the long-run the FC decline to zero.
  - Minimum prices equals the AVC.

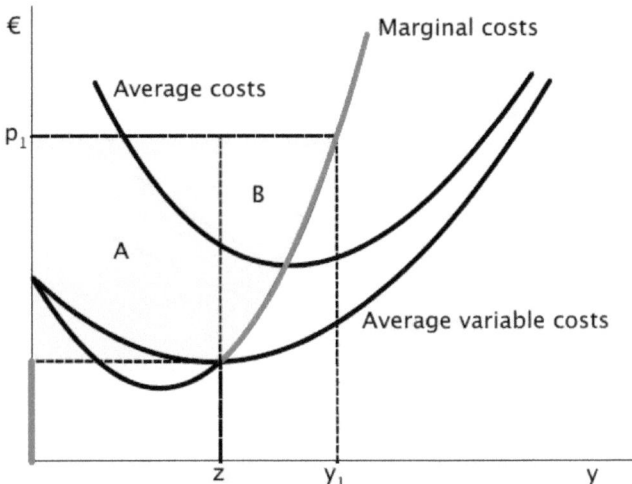

- **Industry supply.**
  - Industry supply is the aggregation of all individual company's supply.
  - The more firms are in the market, the flatter the supply curve is and the more elastic it is.
  - With our model we can figure out / calculate how much companies will be able to enter the market and how many suppliers the market is able to include.
    - In the case of our first demand curve, the price p* is too low for company four and it won't enter / leave the market.
    - If the demand is increasing, then company four is able to enter / stay in the market.
      => In any of these cases point A is observed.

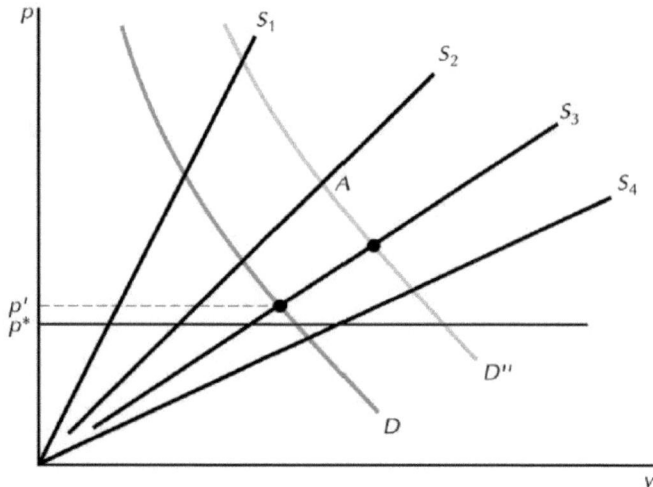

• Assumption of free entry to the market, how does the companies behave?
  • If firms already in the market make profit, others will enter and reduce profits.
  • If firms making losses, they will leave the market and increase profit.
  • Our model just can predict that some companies will leave, not which ones.
  => The equilibrium in the long-run is p = MC = AC → The profit is zero.

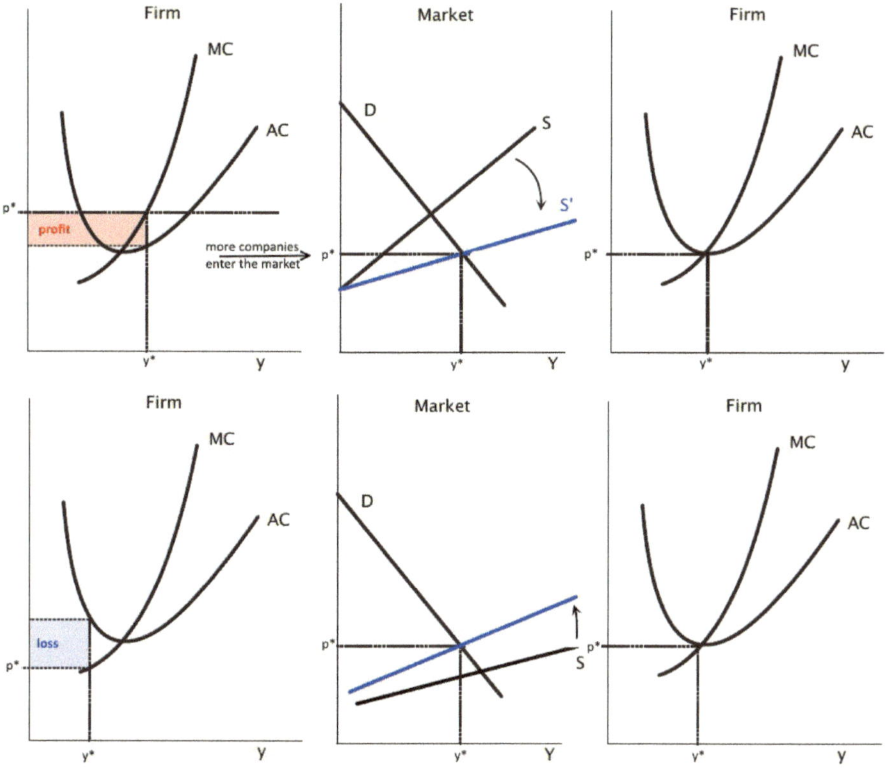

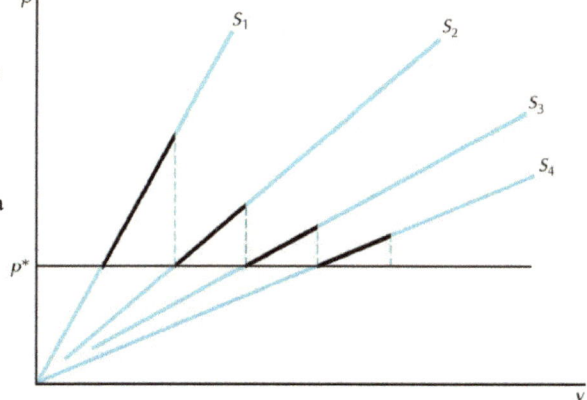

- **The long-run of industry supply.**
  - What is the highest price we can observe in a market until a new company enters and decreases the price?
  - We focus on the part of the supply curve above the price $p*$ but left to the intersect of the next supply curve with the price line.
  - With increasing demand, the price is increasing until its profitable for company X to enter the market followed by a reduction of prices related to increased supply.
    => In the long-run the supply curve is flat, perfectly elastic, elasticity of ∞.
  - Two conditions go hand-in-hand in the pure condition.
    - First condition: Profits are

29

zero (p = AC).
- Second condition: Profits are at their maximum (p = MC).

- **Miscellaneous.**
  - Taxation in the short-run and the long-run.
    - In the short-run the entire tax will be paid totally by producers.
    - In the long-run the tax is completely passed on to consumers.
      => Idea of the British sugar tax.
  - There are barriers to enter, e.g., scarce resources.
  - Companies seem to make profits, but with notice of opportunity costs they aren't.
  - Another company is willing to pay a monthly fee of max. all the profits expected to occur in one period (rent = revenue − variable costs).
    => Owner can decide whether to rent his business and receive the same amount of money with less work or to stay in the business and trying to reduce costs.
  - You have to adjust the average costs to average variable costs and insert a new average costs curve.
  - If companies need licenses for running their business, they could decide to sell them and receive a monthly rent.

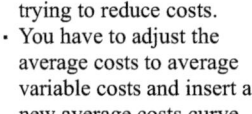
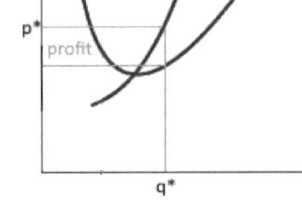
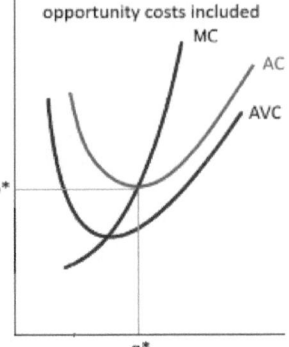

    → License holders have interest in keeping the total amount of licenses small.

- **Summary.**
  - Cost function captures all economically relevant features of production process.
  - Inverse supply of a company is the upward-sloping part of the marginal cost function.
  - Only in the short-run companies can make profits or losses, in the long-run the price is equal to average costs.
  - Pure competition maximizes welfare and total well-being.

- **Monopoly (other extreme case beside pure competition).**
  - Monopolist is the sole seller of one good.
    - Difficult question because the market and the good have to be defined.
    - In the market of Big Macs McDonald's is a monopolist, but in the market of burgers the Big Mac is just one kind of burger (product differentiation).
      => The federal cartel office has to find out / decide whether this is a monopoly or not.

- **Profit maximization of the monopolist.**
  - Consider the following: the company in the pure competition was a price taker and could set quantity as high as possible, the market price won't change. Monopolist only can increase quantity if price is decreasing.
  - $P(y) * y − c(y)$ has to be maximized ($P(y) * y$ takes the consideration from above into account).
  - $P'(y) * y + p(y) = c'(y)$ → Marginal Revenue = Marginal Costs.

- Take elasticity into account.
  - $\varepsilon(y) = y'(p) * p / y(p)$ Inserted in the equation above
  - $p(y) * \left[1 + p_* (y)_* \dfrac{y}{p(y)}\right] = c'(y)$ → $p(y) * \left[1 + \dfrac{1}{\varepsilon(y)}\right] = c'(y)$
- Conclusions from the formula above.
  - The monopolist won't take a price when the demand curve is inelastic.
    - Negative marginal costs aren't wanted.
    - If a price change will lead to a little change in demand, than the price is raised until this effect stops.
  - If elasticity is not equal to infinity, then some market power is given.
  - Inserting infinity in the formula above

$$p(y) * \left[1 + \dfrac{1}{\varepsilon(\infty)}\right] = c'(y) \quad \rightarrow \quad price = marginal\ costs$$

- Related to those formulas the mark-up is the following $\dfrac{\varepsilon(y)}{\varepsilon(y) + 1}$

  - This reveals the factor of MC to get to p*
  - If elasticity is -3 the MC can be exceeded by 1,5 (MC * 1,5 = p*).
    => The more inelastic the demand is, the higher those mark-up.

- **Welfare analysis of a monopoly.**
  - Calculation of marginal revenue.
  - $P(q) = a - b*q$
  - $R(q) = P(q) * q = aq - b*q^2$
  - $R'(q) = a - 2*q$ → The same graph like price (=demand) but with the double slope.
  - **Conclusions from the graphs.**
    - Monopoly price is higher than the competitive market price.
    - Quantity supplied is smaller in a monopoly.
    - Area A turns from consumer's surplus to producer's surplus.
    - Areas B and C are losses.
    - MR is decreasing because increasing quantity requires decreasing price and so the marginal revenue form one unit to another is decreasing.
    => Not Pareto efficient.

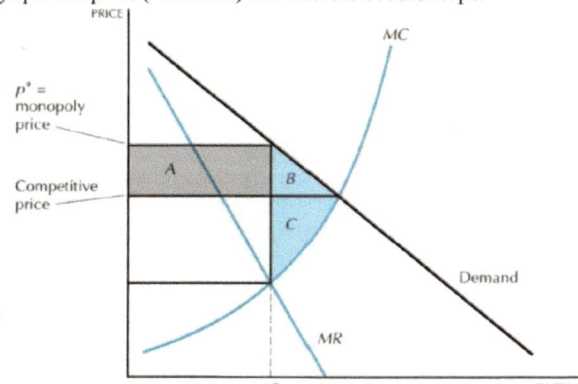

- **Monopoly with price discrimination / differentiation.**
  - Idea of treating one / some person(s) / group(s) differently.
  - Three conditions of price discrimination.
  - **First-degree price discrimination.**
    - Charge a different price for each unit.
    - Turn the consumer's surplus completely into producer's surplus.

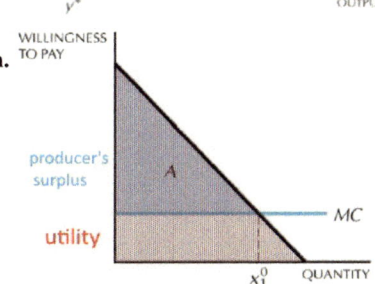

31

- **Second-degree price discrimination.**
  - Same prices for each customer, but different prices for different amounts.
  - Asymmetric information: Company just know that two different types of customers are existing, but can't distinguish them reliably.
  - Offer two different packages, one with less units for the price the basic consumer is willing to pay and another one with more units for a price the premium consumers are willing to pay.
    → Problem: Premium consumers receive greater utility if buying the basis consumer package.
    => Difference in utility received is called rent.
  - Price for the bundle has to be lowered, the premium consumers should receive the same utility if buying basic or premium.
    → Adjust the marginal benefit from the premium consumer to the marginal cost of the basic consumer until they equal.
    => Price and amount have to be reduced to maximize profits.
  - In the figure below area B in graph A is the rent, which should be minimized.
  - In graph B is shown that the marginal benefit is greater than the marginal cost (dark-blue area vs. light-blue one).
  - Figure C shows the optimal amounts and prices for both bundles, rent equals areas B and D, profit A and C.

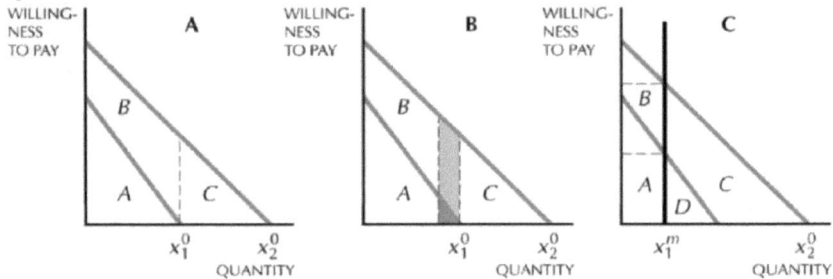

- **Third-degree discrimination.**
  - Different prices for different consumers, but the same price for each good.
  - Two groups are perfectly distinguishable, e.g., offering a student discount only if student ID is shown → allows to interchange the price differenciation.
- **Two-part tariffs.**
  - Price discrimination by offering an entrance fee / regular fixed payment in addition to "lower" prices for usage.
  - In an amusement park you have to pay an entrance fee (full consumer's surplus) and pay additionally for every roller coaster you want to take a ride with (price = marginal costs of producer / provider).

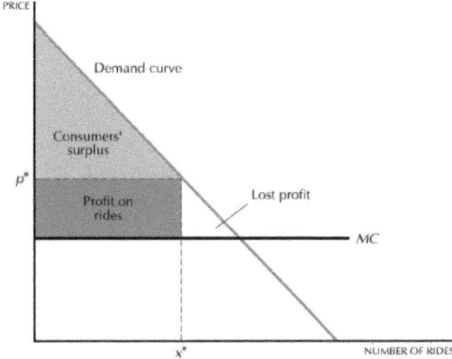

32